THE
TAINTED
GLASS

-ARYA SUDHILAL

It is a common phrase from my hometown,
" If you look through a yellow glass,
The world looks yellow to you "

Dedicated to my parents who have endured me for thirty long years ,

and also my loving husband who encourages me.

CONTENTS

<u>PREFACE</u>

One step forward, two steps back pretty much sums up my life since my early twenties. This is not a motivational book, nor a story with a happily ever after. This book is the world through my tainted glass of schizophrenia.

I always wanted to be a fiction writer. When the clock struck midnight of my thirtieth year of my life on this planet earth, a knight in shining armour did not come searching for me with a perfect glass shoe. Rather, I decided to fit my overgrown foot into a ragged sandal and find out where it took me. Well, the decision was not out of the blue. It took me two to three years of irregular therapy, multiple doctors and two disappointed parents, to realise that my life is a work of fiction; one that my own mind construed up. I thought, I might as well share how the world looked like through the tainted glass of my schizophrenic.

Through this book, I'm hoping to break the stigma associated with schizophrenia and psychosis. It has been a personal journey of courage that made me write this book, with the hope that it aids the ailing silent victims who pretend to be "normal" and endure this silently because of the stigma associated with psychosis and mental illness ,at large. I'm coming out of the closet of "normal".

If our population can be represented using a Gaussian curve, 95.4% of the society falls under the category of "normal". 2.2% on the far right becomes the outstanding members of the society; the ones whom the entire planet aspire to be and the motivational gurus teaches you to be. The 2.2% on the far left, make up the outcasts of the society; the broken and the confused who wish for nothing other than acceptance from the world at large. My book is an ode to the outcasts.

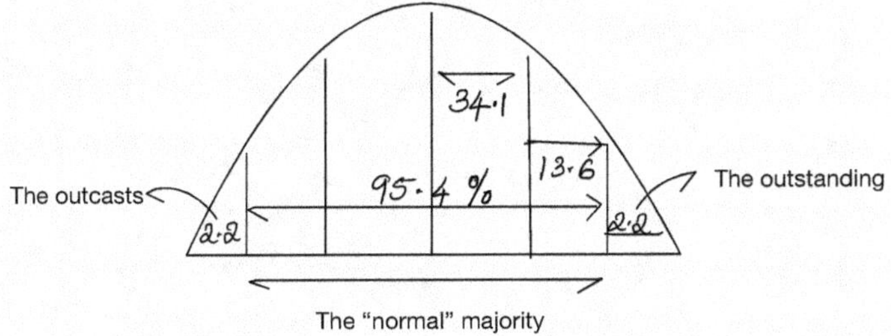

GAUSSIAN CURVE OF POPULATION

<u>**ACKNOWLEDGEMENT**</u>

I deeply express my gratitude to all my readers. I wanted to uplift the down trodden in society. If I achieved my mission, I am grateful.

I would like to thank my parents, my childhood friends who were always there with me, through my highs and lows in life and a special thanks to my therapists, who wish to get me cured, so that I can write up my new chapter in life.

THE GENESIS

I lost my twenties, battling a tough tug-of-war with fantasy and reality, while everyone around me levelled up in life to the third and fourth echelons and I was still in square one.

Five years that I spend in medical school had not taught me to identify symptoms in myself. For someone who aced through high school, it came as a slap, when I started lagging behind in college. I thought that I would catch up with everyone else eventually. No matter how hard I tried, I just could not concentrate. As time went by, I slowly started losing interest in medical science. I could not tell my parents that. As anticipated, I cleared medical school with average marks and attendance.Lagging behind in studies does not necessarily qualify as a symptom of schizophrenia.

We had individual rooms with shared balcony between two adjacent rooms and a common hallway that led to the washrooms in our hostel. Initially, it was my friend from adjacent room with whom I share the balcony, who started talking ill about me. She was almost omnipresent and invariably criticising me. Later, they started ganging up in the common balcony just to say spiteful things about me. I covered up the windows and doors with newspaper, just to stop her from leering at me.

During this time, the loud noise started; of banging doors, music and laughter in the hallways. They clubbed in the hallway to chatter about me. I stopped mingling with people and my friend circle declined to just me in it. One of the girls, who was "jealous " of me started loud music late at night, whenever I tried to sleep. But, I was not going to back away from a challenge. I wrote a heavily worded letter addressing her and dropped it in her room. As expected, when the girls' council gathered, they rounded me up like hyaenas and scolded me till their soul contented.

Even these incidents did not ring any particular bell in my decaying brain that there was something wrong with me and not them. I even confronted one of my friends who kept banging her door "purposefully ". Her reply that the hinge was loose and that she was never in her room, gave me the first hit to my stubborn self-righteous ego.

The second hit came in the form of my biggest hater as I perceived her, came in the form of an angel and prevented me from hanging myself, in time. I was obviously devastated with my academic performance and did not have the maturity in me to understand that a degree was not the end of the universe. She was the first person who suggested that I visit a therapist. I did not feel the need to do so at the time, despite everything that transpired. Added to this was the bigger fear that if I did have some real problem with my psyche, the entire college and teachers would find out. The shame prevented me from seeking help in time.

After somehow graduating from medical school, I worked as a junior resident there for about a month, before I got homesick and came back. But, a bigger disaster awaited me there.

I started entrance coaching for a post graduate degree. As an average or even below average doctor, I could not pull it off in my first or second year after college. There was the added burden of financial struggles in my family. So, I had to work in hospitals and study simultaneously. It was a terrible schedule in my life. I changed hospital after hospital because my salary was meagre and I had the constant feeling that the management and colleagues were conspiring against me. The feeling that there were hidden cameras, made my life miserable. I could not help my family financially with the kind of salary I was getting from these corporate hospitals.

As things were turning from bad to worse, my pre-occupying thought was an easy and painless way to end my life. I tried jumping off the roof my parent's house, I constantly fought with them and I even tried walking off into the night because I could not digest how much I had let everyone down, especially myself.

I was not picking my wounds, but my wounds were becoming lacerations every passing moment. I started feeling that they were mixing things in my food and drinks. Living had become a struggle for me.

THE DIGITAL PANDEMIC

COVID-19 started spreading across the globe or so I read through my multiple Twitter accounts in my phone. With the disease, spread the Internet boom and digital addiction. There was literally nothing to do in the confines of one's room other than "doom-scrolling " Everyone of every age group was busy with their social media. Dopamine has a habit of giving one a temporary high, which eventually becomes a craving. This is true for all addictions, but I am trying to imply the social media addiction here. This is the digital pandemic.

It is said that, the active social media users jumped from 4.62 billion in 2022 to 4.95 billion in 2023. With the pandemic, there was a whooping increase of mental illness, especially depression and anxiety. A study showed that the prevalence of depression increased from 16.2% in the pre- COVID era to 24.6% in the post-COVID period. Along with mood disorders, the incidence of psychosis was also reported to be higher.

During the COVID 19 lockdown, I felt that my phone got hacked. All my social media started talking to me. They leaked all the information about the things I wrote down in digital notepad to general public. Wherever I went, I found people "discussing " the topics which I wrote in my phone. I discarded the "possessed " phone in a well. I started using my parent's phones to access my Twitter account, Facebook and Gmail. Initially, it was an occasional borrowing, later I demanded that my father return the phone that I bought for him just so that I could satiate my internet craving. Now, the reader might think that I'm a selfish person for stooping so low. But, the fact is that you cannot think worse of me than I think of myself. I fought with strangers online to get over my loneliness. As a result, Twitter suspended multiple accounts of mine. I was running out of Gmail IDs to login, so I started using my father's gmail ID to access Twitter.

While on Twitter, I believed that I was making a difference in this world. I developed a feeling that I mattered in an alternate dimension. This helped me get over the feeling of being a complete failure in the real dimension where I lived. This sentiment could be true for any social media influencer; except I was not an influencer. I barely had a handful of followers to whom I shared the little details of my life and my philosophies and aspirations.

I soon started believing that my parent's phones also got hacked because of my incessant trolling. I felt that I put their life in jeopardy. I made up theories about colours, countries, nuclear weapons, women's rights, K-pop, olympics, brands, United Nations among other stuff. All these made perfect sense to me. I could not stop the flow of thoughts. It was like my mind was being bombarded with thoughts. A thousand thoughts came in before one ended. If I were talking to my parents, I would abruptly end conversation and go to the next room to make sense of my endless thoughts. Even when I was driving to hospitals in my two-wheeler, it took a honking truck or bus to snap me out of my reverie. My thoughts were getting dangerous. My parents obviously got worried and took me to a psychiatrist.

THE MEDICATIONS

I was irregular in taking my prescribed medications, because I felt that everything was absolutely fine with me. It is just that no one understood my thoughts. For all I cared, everyone was wrong except me. If they wanted medicines, they can have it.

Initially, I was on risperidone. I started developing a lot of side effects. It felt that the drug was causing more problems than the disease itself. My prolactin level shot up. I developed galactorrhoea. I still don't know if it was the medicine or the disease itself, I had gotten slow in doing things. All my movements were slow and I developed tremors. My eyes started blinking fast; like three or four times the rate of a normal person. There was constant twitching in my eyelids. The worst was the lack of expression on my face. Someone could be cracking up an incredible joke, and I would sit there and stare with the calmness of a monk. There was no expression or reactions. My therapist back then, changed risperidone to aripiprazole and life got a lot better.
I was finding it difficult to keep up with others at work. And one of the hospital that I worked for, even fired me. I was left with no money nor an experience certificate to credit for the hours I put in.

My only companion ever since my twenties was my ego that skyrocketed. An ego that I developed on the name of the prestigious medical school that I graduated from. As time passed by, the prestige of my institution started becoming a burden because I had become one of the handful of graduates from my batch, who did not land a postgraduate degree even on second attempt.

By the grace of god or the devil, I'm still confused over that, I somehow made it into a less demanding postgraduate seat. I am yet to develop an interest in that field. The new college proved to be a bigger nightmare in my life. I was pursuing something that I had no interest in and earning stipend in exchange for nearly twelve hours of my life there. I did not attempt to understand the subject. I believed that I had a bright future if I just crack the entrance and get into surgery. It did not occur to me that, it was a mammoth task for me considering the expertise and knowledge that field demanded and the fact that it took me three years to make it this far.

My colleagues there made a lot of jokes at my expense regarding my "Parkinson's face". I was starting to develop a pathological jealousy towards my colleagues who were doing better than me in studies. It did not occur to me that it is not them that I envied, rather my past self who could do marvels in academics. I was drowning deeper into a sense of shame that I was not measuring up to my own expectations. As my life was becoming a daily joke, I decided that it was time to quit. Enough with degrees and drama, I thought. I will just have to redefine my own values and realise that I am just an average Jane doe who used to be a hard worker. I had to give up my version of the fake legend of yore that I held close to my heart and start from the scratches and bits of self respect that I had left in my life.

Recently, I was started on Aripiprazole and Clozapine. Hopefully, it will eliminate this painful tiny chapter in my life for good. Clozapine, like risperidone also has the risk of extra-pyramidal side effects that I had mentioned before.

<u>**THE IDENTITY CRISIS**</u>

According to Erikson's stages of psychosocial development, there are eight stages that an individual goes through from infancy to adulthood. Each stage had an influence on the succeeding stage.

One major stage is the adolescence, when an individual struggles with one's identity. The pre-occupying question during this time is :

"What am I capable of ?"
Vs
"What does the society expect of me?"

Reconciliation of this problem is necessary for the successful development of adulthood. Erikson coined the term "identity crisis " for an individual incapable of resolving this question harmoniously.Adolescence essentially leads us to a crossroad in our life, where we can choose who we want to be or who the world expects us to be.

Although, I loved to write since childhood in the comfort of my secluded room, I felt the need to be a surgeon since eight, when I had my appendectomy operation. My parents urged me on this quest since it is a trendy and prestigious job. I believed that I was meant to become a surgeon when I aced my exams in school.

The dream slowly started shattering as I reached college and then, it completely went up in flames during my post graduation programme. I was miles away from whom I aspired to be. As a rule of thumb, as our reality and aspirations start parting ways, our ego steps in as a defence mechanism to prevent us from breaking down. It showed me my glorious past and a distorted vision of a grand future. However, our reality cannot catch up with these fantasies. Painfully opening my eyes to reality after ten long years, I see the shattered remains of the grand palace of cards that my ego had constructed. I see my fragile psyche weary and staring at me in disbelief.

Now, at age thirty, I'm at the crossroads contemplating the same existential question that I should have asked myself as an adolescent:

" What am I capable of now as a broke thirty year old?"
Vs
"What does my disappointed and old parents expect of me?"

Now that I have quit my post graduate course to pursue a career that does not pay rent, all my degree certificates remain in the custody of my present college, unless I pay forty lakhs Indian rupees. So, basically I'm presently broke and without a matriculation certificate.

<u>**FOSTERING THE INSANE**</u>

As a child, I have seen my grandfather who had dementia, getting restrained so that he would not run away randomly. Another person who had retired, but his caretakers take care of him like a child; asking him if he used soap while bathing or did he brush his teeth? Yet another woman, who would fight with everyone in the family and one fine morning, she disappeared and no one knows where she is anymore.

All these instances probably made me feel terrible, especially when someone enquires after my health, my parents asking me if I bathed or why I haven't changed my dress in days. It reminds me that I had some kind of mental illness. Despite being a doctor myself, it makes me feel awful when someone treats me like I'm a three year old. My last shards of dignity leaves me.

I assert the fact that I'm not a child and would like to be treated like a thirty year old and be given the freedom that my age demands, such as choosing when to go to bed or how many times I bath in a week. Being treated like I cannot take my own decisions and needs to rely on another person's judgement irritates me. And as any other three year old, I pull tantrums when forced to do something against my will.

When mind becomes our biggest enemy, the word trust in ourselves and our abilities shrinks, until it becomes nonexistent. Added to this is the societal claim that a mentally unfit person is incapable of making even the most insignificant decision on their own. Their judgement of any given situation is considered null and void as per the society and judiciary. It is strange then that I should even entertain the dream of becoming a surgeon. If the world gets to know about my condition, why on earth would they trust their lives or someone they love, in the hands of a doctor who hear voices, has non-existent social skills and more importantly, whom the society has deemed an outcast ? Is it morally correct to even dare to dream about holding a scalpel, when my judgement calls would come under the microscopic scrutiny by the better part of society?

According to WHO, in 2019 about 970 million people globally were diagnosed with a mental disorder. That is, one in every eight people had mental disorder and three per 100 persons were diagnosed with psychotic disorders in their lifetime. That certainly is a lot of people who are banned from dreaming or allowed to make any meaning to their lives. This I believe is the real reason people stay hidden under the blanket cover of normality.

"Understanding is the first step to acceptance,
And only with acceptance can there be recovery"
-J K Rowling

<u>**IDENTIFYING THE SYMPTOMS EARLY**</u>

I bored you initially with my short autobiography, because I was hoping that you could make out the difference in my thinking pattern from others. I was giving you a look through the tainted glass of schizophrenia. My world is filled with enemies who wish me harmed. It is hard living through every day feeling that someone somewhere is plotting against you. The hardest thing for me to do is trust anyone, for how do you trust another, when you can't trust your own thoughts and senses?

Schizophrenia has prodromal phase, positive and negative symptoms. (Just naming a few)

The positive symptoms includes,
*Visual hallucinations- seeing things that are not there
*Auditory hallucinations- hearing things that are not there
*Olfactory hallucinations- smell that is not there
*Delusions - false fixed beliefs

The negative symptoms includes,
*Avolition - decreased initiation of goal directed behaviour
*Alogia - inability to speak
*Anhedonia - lack of interest in things that you once enjoyed
*Social withdrawal

Nonspecific symptoms such as
*Disorganised speech

It is good to understand and look out for the symptoms that I have briefly described.
But, it is necessary to consult a therapist, before making a self-diagnosis. Identifying the symptoms early aids in better outcome of the disease.

From my narrative of what happened in my past, I could
understand that I have :

 #Delusion of reference (that people are speaking of me)
#Delusion of persecution (that people are out to get me)
#I had flight of ideas during my psychosis (thought
bombardment)
#Social withdrawal
#Avolition (I couldn't even put on gloves properly)

These are just my own identification of symptoms based on
a retrospective examination of my self.

Despite the diagnosis, I just could not bring myself to take
the medication.

Through my story, you might have even identified the five
stages of insight :
01) Complete denial of illness
02) slight awareness, but still denying
03) awareness present, but blaming on external factors
04) intellectual insight
05) emotional insight

Perhaps I have only reached the fourth stage of insight as
of now. But, I'm taking my medication regularly ever since
my doctor told me, I could eventually have brain atrophy, if I
don't take my medication regularly.

<u>**FREEDOM**</u>

Long have I tried to fit in this society,
Pretending to fit in all the boxes,
Painted myself in colours of their choice,
Long I prayed for societal acceptance,
Having denied myself the dignity,
The acceptance of my uniqueness,
My colour, my flair, my boundless mind,
Long have I denied the redemption of self acceptance.
I know my words do not rhyme,
For that is my freedom, my style.

— ARYA SUDHILAL

LETTING GO OF THE LEGEND OF YORE

Often, we are so caught up in the vision of what we want to be and our past, that we refuse to look beyond; at the present. The reality can be presented with so much distortion by our ego, that we stop looking for anything else.

We have to stop dwelling on our past and the fantasies fabricated by our ego as a defense mechanism to protect us from the harshness of reality. Unless our memories of past glory and regrets die in us, birth of new ideas cannot happen. Life is a cycle of creation and destruction, until our last breath. We have to embrace the joy of creation, and the pain of destruction equally. We cannot hold onto one and let go of the other, just because it is too painful.

Life can be compared to an alternating current curve, with upstrokes and downstrokes. It keeps alternating between positive and negative.

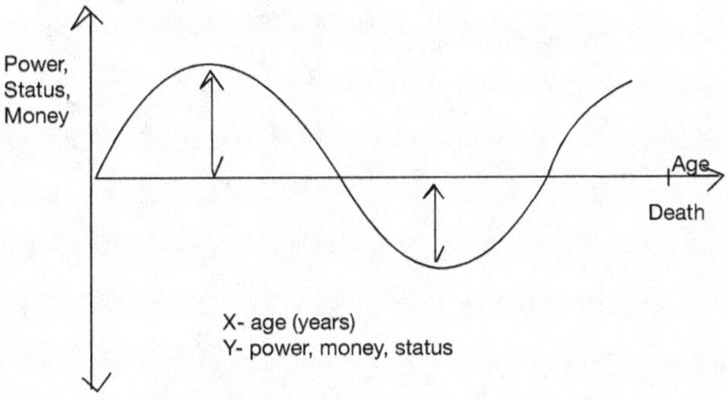

Life Trend Curve

Variables like status, money, power, fame keep changing over time, while our age keeps progressing. Holding on to these variables that are momentary and refusing to live in the reality , prevents us from seeing the only approaching constant; death.The reality of these transient variables is that they are mere illusion. The control that we may feel over money, status and power is like holding onto a reflection in the mirror; it shows us what we want to see.

Even when our lives seem to be climbing the peak of Everest or taking a nosedive into the Mariana Trench, if we are able to maintain a sense of stability of mindset, we have attained the middle ground that Lord Buddha advocated. We have to convert the AC current curve in life, to that of a Direct current curve ,that is stable and linear, we have attained middle path. All we have to do is to turn on the rectifier of life.

We become unstoppable, when we realise the need for destruction of our old and decaying thoughts and lifestyle ,to make way for the new.

Defeat, my defeat
My deathless courage,
You and I shall laugh together with the storm,
And together we shall dig graves for all that die in us,
And we shall stand in the sun with a will
And we shall be dangerous

   - Kahlil Gibran

Thank you for reading.